WHAT IS FATE?

Some say life is like a river, with both smooth waters and wild rapids, and we are tossed upon its currents. We might encounter sunshine or torrential rain on our way. We might glide gently through a peaceful valley but then enter a raging whirlpool and feel trapped. Sometimes the river flows clearly onward. At other times, it twists and turns, taking us in unexpected directions.

That is what fate is. For better or worse, we have to deal with whatever fate gives us. When we hit a snag in this river, most of us are frightened and helpless, letting life's whirlpools suck us under. But some people struggle against the current with courage and determination.

Ludwig van Beethoven was such a person because he struggled against the gradual loss of his hearing. For a musician, there is nothing more tragic. A deaf musician is like a painter without fingers, a soccer player without feet. Beethoven could not hear the sound of musical instruments or the pitch of a single note. Although his fate challenged him, miraculously, his best works were completed after he went deaf.

Beethoven triumphed over life's tragedies and his own suffering. He achieved the impossible by creating powerful music in his world of silence. He is a hero, a hero who fought against the limitations of his fate.

Mason Crest Publishers, Inc.
370 Reed Road
Broomall, Pennsylvania 19008
866-MCP-BOOK (toll free)

Illustrations copyright © 2001
Vitali P. Konstantinov
Published in association with
Grimm Press Ltd., Taiwan

1 3 5 7 9 8 6 4 2

Library of Congress Cataloging-in-
Publication Data:

on file at the Library of Congress.

ISBN 1-59084-148-4
ISBN 1-59084-133-6 (series)

Great Names

BEETHOVEN

Mason Crest Publishers
Philadelphia

Ludwig van Beethoven was born one winter's day in 1770 in Bonn, Germany.

Several members of Beethoven's family were important musicians. His grandfather was the music master at the court in Bonn. His father, Johann, was made one of the court's singers at the age of 12. Musicians often visited the Beethoven home, and beautiful music was always drifting from the windows.

Because Beethoven grew up in a world of music, he naturally followed a musical path. When Beethoven was still a small child, fate knocked on his door.

Beethoven's father, Johann, began to drink heavily. This destroyed his voice, which made him earn less money. In response, Johann turned his disappointment in himself into high expectations for his son. Johann became very determined that Ludwig would be a child prodigy, a second Mozart. He wanted to train Ludwig's talent, and then travel with the boy around Europe doing recitals, in order to receive the patronage of the court.

And so Beethoven's unhappy childhood began. His father made him practice the piano every day, even though he was still not big enough to reach the keyboard. He had to stand on the piano stool to play. At times, his father would even wake him up in the middle of the night to practice. But what Beethoven hated most was that he had to play the music exactly as it was written or his father would punish him severely.

"Why do I have to play it this way?" Beethoven would think angrily. "Why can't I play it the way I want to?" His happiest moments were when his father was not there. Then he would ignore the written music and play as he wished. But if his father found out, he would be punished again.

When Beethoven was just eight years old, his father arranged for his first concert. The court in Bonn was very impressed with the young musician. Germany already had a Mozart. Who would have thought there would be another? The court decided to support Beethoven. It also decided that Beethoven needed a better tutor than his father.

Fate then led Beethoven to meet his first mentor, Christian Neefe. Neefe's teaching style was completely different from that of Johann Beethoven. Neefe allowed Beethoven to feel the beauty of the music he played. Neefe not only taught his pupil to sight-read but also stirred his passion for music. When Beethoven was just 12 years old, Neefe recommended him as an assistant at the court. With his teacher's guidance, Beethoven blossomed.

In the meantime, his father's performances became worse and worse. The Court kept cutting his wages and increasing Beethoven's. Before long, Beethoven was supporting his drunken father, his sickly mother, and two younger brothers. His talented fingers had a heavy burden to bear.

Beethoven studied the violin, cello, organ, and other instruments, as well as the piano.

When he was 17, Beethoven went to Vienna. There, he studied music with the financial support of the Grand Duke of Austria and performed in front of Mozart. Mozart soon accepted Beethoven as a student.

In 1787, Beethoven's mother passed away. Beethoven returned to Bonn and worked very hard performing, teaching, and taking care of his family. He had

little time for much else. At this time, the opening shots had been fired in the French Revolution. Democratic ideas were spreading all over Europe. These ideas stirred Beethoven's hunger for independence. He did not want to keep performing for the aristocracy. He wanted to play and compose in freedom.

When Beethoven returned to Vienna, he added his own genius to the music he performed. His audiences were thrilled, sometimes even moved to tears. His unique style soon conquered the music capital of Vienna, and Beethoven became its biggest star since Mozart.

"Brilliant! Brilliant!" Everyone was talking about him and wanted him to come and perform for them. His compositions were also selling very well.

As time went on, Beethoven stopped playing other composers' works so that he could focus on composing his own. He wrote sonata after sonata, concerto after concerto.

Until then, composers had tried to create beauty and harmony in their music, but this wasn't enough for Beethoven.

He wanted to express powerful feelings in his music. His compositions were beautiful, as if sent from heaven like the ancient fire of Prometheus, which filled the world with light.

Just as Beethoven was at the peak of his powers, fate knocked on his door once again. He discovered that there was something wrong with his hearing. At first, there was only a slight twanging in his ears, but later, this turned into a constant ringing.

How was he to compose or perform if he could not hear the sound of musical instruments or the pitch of a note? Afraid to let anyone know what was happening to him, he kept his suffering to himself. Beethoven left Vienna and went to stay in the countryside where he hoped to keep his problem a secret. The peace and beauty of the countryside helped to calm him. It also helped him compose several more works.

More important, he fell in love with Countess Guillietta Guicciardi and wrote the famous *Moonlight Sonata* for her.

But his illness continued to eat away inside him. As his hearing got worse, so did his state of mind. As a result, he gave up his romance.

The loss of his love and his hearing made life unbearable. One day, as he was walking with one of his students, a beautiful song could be heard in the distance. But Beethoven could hear nothing.

He later wrote with grief: "O, all of you who think I'm unkind or stubborn or crazy, you do me wrong. You do not know the secret cause of my condition. . . . How can I say to you, 'Speak louder, shout, for I am deaf.' . . . My hearing should be sharper than anyone else's. How can I admit that I hear nothing?"

Yet Beethoven refused to give up, and he recovered his determination, saying, "I must take fate by the throat. It shall not crush me entirely."

At this time, revolutionary ideas were
spreading from France throughout Europe. Napoleon, the French
leader, was bringing his country toward freedom and equality. As
the new hero of Europe, Napoleon inspired Beethoven. He started
to compose a symphony in the hero's honor, which he called the *Eroica*
(the *Heroic Symphony*). But just as Beethoven was completing the work, Napoleon
abandoned his democratic ideas and had himself crowned as emperor.

Beethoven could not believe the news. He asked everyone to repeat it loudly in his ear. Once he was sure of Napoleon's betrayal, he shouted angrily: "But he's only a common little man. . . . He has trampled all over our human rights. His unchecked ambition will make him a tyrant." And so Beethoven tore up his symphony's dedication page.

Since his struggle with deafness began, Beethoven had spent much time in the countryside. In all sorts of weather, he would go out walking; the countryside inspired him, especially the power of thunderstorms. They crashed down on him like his fate, blow after blow: first, his harsh father, then, the loss of his mother and the difficult years that followed, and now, his tormenting illness. Yet he would not give in. Instead, he used his struggle and his pain creatively and wrote passionate music. He worked very slowly and carefully to craft his compositions. With the help of a hearing aid, he wrote note after note, which he probably couldn't hear. In this manner, Beethoven wrote the *Fifth Symphony*. Its theme reflects his life: being fearless in the face of fate's challenges, standing firm as the thunder crashes and the rain pours down.

FREIHEIT UEBER ALLES LIEBEN

This symphony, along with the *Eroica*, spread Beethoven's fame throughout Europe. Soon, he rose to the ranks of the leading composers.

Gradually, Beethoven lost his hearing completely. At this point, people could communicate with him only through writing. He carried a notebook with him everywhere. If someone wanted to talk to him, he or she would write down a comment or question, and Beethoven would respond.

Playing the piano eventually became a nightmare. When he played a note softly, he had no way of knowing whether it made any sound at all. These problems changed his personality, and he became more and more irritable. He stopped caring about his

appearance, leaving his hair wild and uncombed and his clothes torn and rumpled. If his cook prepared something he didn't like, he would smash the bowl. If his students wrote weak compositions, he would angrily tear up their manuscripts.

Beethoven took great care to avoid crowds of people and grew more and more distant from his close friends. He became fearful of others, which caused him to move his home frequently and change his staff often. It was as if he were living in a dense fog.

He was at his most depressed when he met the famous poet, Johann Goethe, whom he much admired. At first, this friendship brought a ray of light into his life. But they were not to remain friends, as their personalities were too different. Once, when they were out walking, a royal carriage passed by them. Goethe hurried to the side of the road and bowed. But Beethoven turned his back and slowly strolled away. Not surprisingly, the two men drifted apart.

In 1815, Beethoven's brother suddenly died, leaving him and his sister-in-law as joint guardians for his nine-year-old nephew, Karl. After several years of fighting over custody, Beethoven won. Although he loved his nephew dearly, he knew very little about raising a child, and they often quarreled. Heartbroken, he struggled to write any music at all.

At the same time, the musical tastes in Vienna began to change. The new favorite was the composer Rossini. Beethoven's music seemed serious and dark in comparison. With many of his former patrons and friends either dead or gone, Beethoven became more and more isolated. In 1816, he wrote in his diary, "I have no friends. I am alone in the world."

Once, when conducting his opera, *Fidelio*, he waved the baton so wildly that the orchestra became totally confused and had to stop playing. One of his friends wrote in Beethoven's notebook: "Please don't continue conducting. It would be better if you went home." When he read this, Beethoven jumped up like a wounded animal and dashed out with a great cry.

"Shall I just give up?" Once again, Beethoven found himself questioning his fate. But he remembered the words of the poem, *Ode to Joy*, written by his friend, Friedrich Schiller. He realized that if he could not hear the world outside, then he must listen to the music within.

Determined to look for joy beyond suffering, he painstakingly wrote the *Ninth Symphony*, the chorus of which uses the words of Schiller's poem.

Beethoven insisted on conducting the *Ninth Symphony* himself, saying he could do it by watching the actions of the orchestra. At the end of the performance, the audience gave him a standing ovation.

PLAUDITE AMICI, COMOEDIA

FINITA EST

Because he couldn't hear it, one of the singers had to turn him around before he was aware of the cheering.

Beethoven had yet to face one last twist of fate. In 1826, his beloved nephew Karl attempted to shoot himself. Although Karl survived, this event hit Beethoven hard. His health began to fail, and the day came when he could no longer get out of bed.

On March 26, 1827, a northerly wind brought storms to Vienna. Beethoven's strong hands became limp, his breathing stopped, and he died.

In his lifetime, Beethoven wrote nine symphonies and dozens of sonatas and concertos. Every piece forms an important part of our musical tradition. Beethoven is honored along with Bach and Mozart as one of the greatest composers the world has ever known.

His deafness was a terrible tragedy, yet he wrote his finest works after he lost his hearing. Beethoven's life could be described as a symphony written in suffering and sadness but played with great courage and strength.

BIOGRAPHY

Author Anna Carew-Miller is a freelance writer and former teacher who lives in rural northwestern Connecticut with her husband and daughter. Although she has a Ph.D. in American Literature and has done extensive research and writing on literary topics, more recently, Anna has written books for younger readers, including reference books and middle reader mysteries.